OUT OF THIS WORLD

Meet NASA Inventor William "Red" Whittaker
and His Team's

Alien Cave Explorers

WORLD BOOK

www.worldbook.com

World Book, Inc.
180 North LaSalle Street
Suite 900
Chicago, Illinois 60601
USA

For information about other World Book publications, visit our website at www.worldbook.com or call 1-800-WORLDBK (967-5325).

For information about sales to schools and libraries, call 1-800-975-3250 (United States), or 1-800-837-5365 (Canada).

Library of Congress Cataloging-in-Publication Data for this volume has been applied for.

Out of This World
978-0-7166-6155-9 (set, hc.)

Alien Cave Explorers
ISBN: 978-0-7166-6163-4 (hc.)

Also available as:
ISBN: 978-0-7166-6172-6 (e-book)

Printed in China by Shenzhen Donnelley Printing Co., Ltd., Guangdong Province
1st printing June 2017

Staff

Writer: Jeff De La Rosa

Executive Committee

President
Jim O'Rourke

Vice President and
Editor in Chief
Paul A. Kobasa

Vice President, Finance
Donald D. Keller

Vice President, Marketing
Jean Lin

Vice President, International Sales
Maksim Rutenberg

Director, Human Resources
Bev Ecker

Editorial

Director of Print Content
Developemnt
Tom Evans

Editor, Print Content Development
Kendra Muntz

Managing Editor, Science
Jeff De La Rosa

Editor, Science
William D. Adams

Librarian
S. Thomas Richardson

Manager, Contracts & Compliance
(Rights & Permissions)
Loranne K. Shields

Manager, Indexing Services
David Pofelski

Administrative Assistant, Digital
and Print Content Development
Ethel Matthews

Digital

Director, Digital Content
Development
Emily Kline

Director, Digital Product
Development
Erika Meller

Manager, Digital Products
Jonathan Wills

Graphics and Design

Senior Art Director
Tom Evans

Senior Visual Communications
Designer
Melanie Bender

Media Researcher
Rosalia Bledsoe

Manufacturing/ Production

Manufacturing Manager
Anne Fritzinger

Proofreader
Nathalie Strassheim

Contents

4 Introduction

8 Caves

10 Lava tubes

12 INVENTOR FEATURE:

Spelunker (and what's in a name)

14 Locating caves

16 A campaign of exploration

18 Stage one: Orbital scouting

22 Stage two: Scouting by aerial and surface craft

26 INVENTOR FEATURE: Jules Verne

28 Stage three: Descending into the pit

30 BIG IDEA: The Tyrolean traverse

32 INVENTOR FEATURE: Mother of invention

34 Stage four: Underground exploration

36 BIG IDEA: Seeing in the dark

38 INVENTOR FEATURE: Farmer Red

40 Why study caves?

42 BIG IDEA: Future cave dwellers

44 Red Whittaker and his team

45 Glossary

46 For further information/Think like an inventor

47 Index

48 Acknowledgments

Glossary There is a glossary of terms on page 45. Terms defined in the glossary are in boldface type that **looks like this** on their first appearance on any spread (two facing pages).

Pronunciations (how to say words) are given in parentheses the first time some difficult words appear in the book. They look like this: pronunciation (pruh NUHN see AY shuhn).

Introduction

Over the past 50 years, scientists have learned a lot about the various rocky worlds that make up our **solar system.** Spacecraft in orbit have photographed and mapped in great detail the surfaces of the moon and of the planets Mars, Venus, and Mercury. In the 1960's and 1970's, human explorers walked on the surface of the moon. A series of *missions* (special tasks) in the late 1990's and early 2000's used **rovers** to land directly on the surface of Mars. The images these rovers sent back to Earth have completely changed our understanding of Mars.

All this exploration has been only skin deep, so to speak. To truly understand an *alien* (unknown) world, we must dig beneath its surface. Drilling even a few feet or meters into an alien world would be a difficult and costly job. Perhaps there is another way.

Some objects in the solar system, such as the moon, may have vast cave networks beneath their surfaces.

Since the early 2000's, advances in imaging technology have revealed hundreds of pits opening into the surface of the solar system's rocky worlds. There is evidence that many of these pits may connect to underground caves.

Caves on other planets offer the promise of untold scientific treasures. Think about the caves of Mars, for example. The surface of Mars is a cold, dry place. Scientists know that there is water on Mars, but nearly all of it lies beneath the surface. Also, conditions on Mars may have once been more favorable for supporting living things. If life ever developed on Mars, it may have retreated underground as the environment on the surface grew harsh. Whether scientists are searching for water or for evidence of life on Mars, caves may be a great place to look.

Engineer William "Red" Whittaker wants to send robots to enter pits on objects in space and explore any caves they find. But exploring alien caves will not be easy.

Caves present an astonishing variety of complex and difficult **terrain.** And because caves are hidden from view, cave explorers will not know what challenges they will have until they enter the caves. Robotic cave explorers will also have to operate in darkness, without the benefit of **solar power** or direct communication with scientists here on Earth.

Even with these challenges, the mission would be worthwhile. There is more at stake than simple curiosity. Many of our ancient ancestors lived in caves for the natural shelter they provide. If people are ever to live on the moon or Mars, they may need to rely on caves to protect themselves and their equipment from the dangerous conditions.

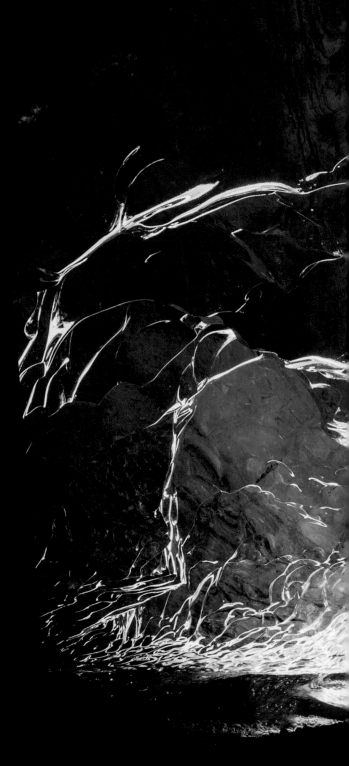

The NASA Innovative Advanced Concepts program.  The titles in the *Out of This World* series feature projects that have won grant money from a group formed by the United States National Aeronautics and Space Administration, or NASA. The NASA Innovative Advanced Concepts program (NIAC) provides funding to teams working to develop bold new advances in space technology. You can visit NIAC's website at www.nasa.gov/niac.

Meet Red Whittaker.

❚❚ Hello, I'm Red Whittaker, **engineer** and professor of robotics at Carnegie Mellon University in Pittsburgh, Pennsylvania. When I was a child, I got into holes and caverns all the time. Now I am working to develop robotic missions to explore caves on the moon and Mars. ❚❚

7

Caves

A cave is a natural hollow, or space, in the ground that is large enough for a person to enter. Some caves consist of a single *chamber* (roomlike space) only a few yards or meters deep. Other caves include large networks of passages and chambers. The longest cave ever explored is the Mammoth-Flint Ridge cave system in Kentucky, in the central United States. This cave has about 340 miles (550 kilometers) of explored passageways, but scientists think that it extends even farther.

Most caves on Earth are solution caves. Solution caves are formed by the action of water. The water trickles through the ground, dissolving limestone or similar rock. Over thousands or millions of years, the water eats away at the rock, carving passages, chambers, and pits. Eventually, the rock above part of the cave may collapse, forming a vertical entrance called a *sinkhole*. A horizontal entrance may develop on a hillside or a valley slope, especially where water flows from the cave.

The interior of a solution cave is a damp, dark place where sunlight never enters. Explorers using artificial lights may discover a strange underground landscape filled with beautiful, oddly shaped mineral deposits such as *stalactites* and *stalagmites*. Stalactites are iciclelike formations that hang from the ceiling of a cave. Stalagmites are pillars that rise from the floor. Many caves also have underground lakes, rivers, and waterfalls.

Most caves on Earth, such as this one in the Central American country of Belize, are formed by the action of water.

9

Lava tubes

Water is much less plentiful on the other rocky worlds of our **solar system.** On dry worlds, such as the moon, most caves are probably lava tubes. Lava tubes are formed by the action of flowing lava. The lava may come from an erupting volcano.

" The lava may also come from a big impact. A huge **meteorite** hits the moon or Mars, and there is so much energy that it just melts the rock, right into a big puddle. " —Red

Like water, lava flows downhill, forming rivers of melted, or molten, rock. As the lava flows, it cools, causing the rock to harden. The rock cools and hardens from the outside in, forming a crust or lid.

" It is similar to the way some rivers here on Earth freeze in winter. The surface of the river hardens into ice, but there is still liquid water flowing underneath. " —Red

In the same way, the lava continues to flow through a tube beneath the hardened cover. Eventually, the volcano stops erupting, or the lava from the impact drains away.

" The lava continues to flow out through the tube, but there is no longer any lava flowing in to replace it. When that happens, the lava level inside the tube goes down and down and down and down. " —Red

Eventually, all the lava flows out, and the crust of rock hardens entirely. The entire process leaves behind a long, narrow, tube-shaped cave—a lava tube.

Lava tubes are found on Earth in places where there is volcanic activity. Earth has the strongest gravitational pull of the rocky worlds in our solar system. Earth's gravitation pulls on flowing and hardening lava, limiting the size to which lava tubes can grow.

The gravitational pulls of the moon and of Mars, on the other hand, are much, much weaker. As a result, lava tubes can grow to enormous size.

❚❚ The physics of low gravity allows these lava tubes to grow wider, taller, and in some cases much longer than any that we know of on Earth. **❚❚** —Red

Scientists explore a lava tube in this photograph (left).

A lava tube may remain hidden beneath the surface until part of its roof collapses suddenly, forming an opening called a skylight.

Sinkholes

Lava tubes are not the only caves whose roofs can collapse suddenly. Solution caves collapse to form openings called sinkholes. In 2014, a large sinkhole opened overnight beneath the U.S. National Corvette Museum in Bowling Green, Kentucky, swallowing eight of the classic Chevrolet cars!

Inventor feature:
Spelunker (and what's in a name)

From an early age, Red Whittaker showed an interest in underground exploration.

❝ I grew up in the Allegheny Mountains west of Pittsburgh, Pennsylvania, in a setting where I could get out in the woods and climb and get into water, get into holes. We even had something called a *root cellar*. It is basically a little cave near your house, and that is where people used to store apples and potatoes and things like that for the winter. **❞** —Red

As Whittaker got older, this interest developed into a hobby of *spelunking* (exploring caves) and mountaineering.

❝ That was a major hobby at one time. I would get into bigger and more interesting caves and mountains and enjoyed all that. **❞** —Red

As a child, William Whittaker picked up the nickname "Red," in reference to his red hair.

> ❝ I think almost every red-headed kid in America gets called 'Red.' I resisted it for a long while. ❞ —Red

Whittaker eventually embraced the nickname, and it stuck. He's still called "Red" even though his red hair is long gone.

> ❝ Now I use it for everything. I sign checks with it. I do business with it. I'm Red Whittaker. That is me. ❞ —Red

Locating
caves

The scientific study of alien caves took off in the early 2000's with advances in high-**resolution** imaging. For images taken from orbit, the higher the resolution, the easier it is to see small features.

In 2009, scientists began to identify open pits in high-resolution images of the moon and Mars. Some of these images show details down to a few feet or meters across, but it is not always easy for scientists to tell what they are looking at. Scientists identify pits and other features in such images by looking closely at areas of sunlight and shadow.

|| If there is a bump or a hill, it will be lit up on the sunny side and shadowed on the opposite side. Looking right down on a pit, on the other hand, you see a more or less circular shadow. There is a just a tiny arc of illumination on the rim opposite the sun, a little bit like a crescent moon. **||** —Red

Orbiting space probes, such as the U.S. Lunar Reconnaissance Orbiter, launched in 2009, map the surfaces of their targets in great detail. Such probes produce huge volumes of high-resolution imagery.

Scientists use special computer software to look for telltale patterns of light and dark.

❚❚ The computer spits out lots and lots of potential hits, images that could show a pit. A human being has to look at the image to verify them. **❚❚** —Red

Amateur cave sleuths

Much high-resolution surface imagery is available for anyone to see, enabling *amateur* (not professional) explorers to participate in the hunt for possible caves. In 2010, students at Evergreen Middle School in Cottonwood, California, discovered a large skylight (pictured below) on the slopes of the Martian volcano Pavonis Mons. The students were working with NASA scientists as part of the Mars Student Imaging Project.

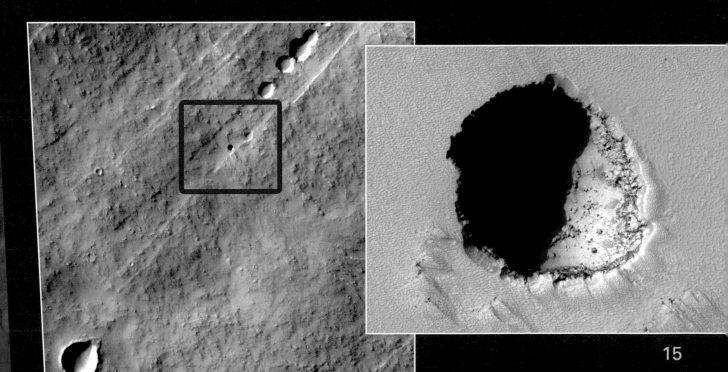

A campaign of
exploration

Exploring an alien cave is not as simple as just sending a **rover** to enter one of these pits. For one thing, most rovers so far have been designed to operate on fairly flat, even ground. In fact, mission planners tend to select landing sites in areas free of pits, slopes, and other features to avoid damaging or stranding their craft.

Whittaker's robotic cave explorers, on the other hand, will have to make exact landings near their target pits. Entering a pit presents an even greater challenge. Pits and caves are complex environments, filled with broken pieces of rock and other obstacles.

❝ Some of these pits have *vertical* [straight up and down] walls, or even *overhung walls* [walls that hang over the pit]. Some may feature more gentle, ramplike slopes that go all the way from the surface down to the bottom. ❞ —Red

Taking the image from orbit does not necessarily solve this problem. There is also a limit to what can be determined about a pit from orbital imagery. Any caves that connect to the pit, for example, may be hidden from orbital view entirely. Mission planners will not know what challenges a robotic explorer will face until they get a closer look.

" That is the thing about exploration: a lot of times, you do not really know what you are up against until you are there. **"** —Red

So it may be impossible to explore a cave with a single mission. Rather, alien caves will likely require repeated exploration.

" Here on Earth, explorers once longed to reach the South Pole or to climb Mount Everest. That did not mean it was easy or that it happened the first time. Alien caves are worth exploring, but they are going to require a number of missions and explorations over time. **"** —Red

These missions might consist of several stages, including (1) orbital scouting, (2) scouting by *aerial* (in the air) and surface craft, (3) descending into the pit, and (4) underground exploration of any caves found.

Stage one: Orbital scouting

A mission of alien cave exploration begins with scouting, or looking, for a location while the spacecraft is in orbit. Once a pit has been identified in surface imagery, spacecraft that orbit the moon or planet can be directed to take a closer look.

Mission planners can learn much about a pit by studying orbital imagery. A computerized image is made up of a grid of little squares called *pixels*. The size of a pixel is related to the resolution of the image. At a certain resolution, for example, one pixel might represent one square meter of surface. So by counting pixels, mission planners can determine the size of a pit.

By measuring shadows, trained researchers can also estimate a pit's depth. They may get a sense of a pit's interior by

❚❚ The pits we have identified [on the moon and Mars] so far vary in size. A few are the size of a professional sports stadium. The smallest ones we can see are about the size of a house. ❚❚ —Red

analyzing variations in brightness within an image. Smooth surfaces tend to vary little in brightness. Rough, rubble-strewn surfaces, on the other hand, show many contrasts of light and shadow.

Orbiting spacecraft may even take *stereoscopic* images of a pit. In this technique, the craft takes two images from slightly different angles. Combining the images shows the depth of major features, providing a three-dimensional view of the pit.

All of this information helps mission managers to select a cave to explore and a safe landing site nearby. It also helps them to decide which kind of robot will be needed to descend into the pit.

❚❚ Some of these pictures are so good, you can look down in there and actually see boulders and the parts of the roof that fell in. **❚❚** —Red

A spacecraft can gather more information about a pit if it is able to photograph it under different lighting conditions. The above images are pictures of the same lunar pit at different times. The sun has illuminated different parts of the walls and floor of the pit in each image.

Of course, there are many different ways for scientists to look for underground caves, even from orbit.

❚❚ I said you could not see underground caves from orbit. That is true for small caves. But you can discover much bigger caves by making detailed measurements of gravity. ❚❚ —Red

An object's gravitational pull is related to its **mass.** The more mass, the stronger the gravitational pull. Imagine an orbiting probe measuring the gravitational pull of the moon. The probe detects a drop in gravitational pull over a certain area. The drop indicates that the mass of that part of the moon is less. An underground cave could account for the missing mass.

In 2012, two orbiters made just such detailed observations of the moon's gravity as part of NASA's GRAIL mission. (*GRAIL* stands for *Gravity Recovery and Interior Laboratory.*)

❚❚ In 2016, scientists studying the GRAIL data discovered evidence of a vast underground cave. It is kind of long and narrow, shaped like a loaf of Italian bread. It appears to be about half the size of Manhattan [an island that makes up much of New York City]. ❚❚ —Red

In 2012, the GRAIL mission completed this gravity field map of the moon's surface. Red indicates excess mass which creates areas of higher gravity, and blue corresponds to less mass which creates areas of lower gravity.

21

Stage two: Scouting by aerial and surface craft

❝ There are detailed imagery and other measurements for the entire surface of the moon and of Mars, in some cases down to **resolutions** below 3 feet [1 meter]. You can look down and see all the previous **rovers** and **landers** sent to Mars. You can even see the walking trails of astronauts on the moon. But from orbit, you can never see into a cave. **❞** —Red

To discover any caves connected to a pit, scientists will have to send robotic explorers for a closer look. A first step might be to send a robotic craft to fly over the pit at close range. Whittaker thinks that such a flyover examination could be carried out by a lander. As the craft descends to the surface, it would pass over the pit at low altitude, taking detailed images of the pit interior.

After landing near the pit, the craft could release a surface rover. The rover would approach the pit, conducting detailed examinations from the pit's rim.

In this illustration, a lander descends to explore a lunar pit.

❚❚ The first surface missions will likely use driving robots, not too different from the rovers being used right now. These rovers will get to these great pits and take the first look. ❚❚ —Red

Pit exploration will require a few changes to the way rovers are designed now. For one thing, most rovers are designed for close examination of their nearest surroundings.

A pit-scouting rover, on the other hand, will require more long-range instruments. It will likely have to look tens or even hundreds of feet or meters down and across from the pit's edge.

❝ From a robot's eye view, it will be almost like coming upon the Grand Canyon. ❞ —Red

Information gathered by the pit-scouting rover will help determine whether or not the pit connects to any underground caves. It will also aid in the design of a rover that can enter the pit. Once its observations are complete, mission managers may even consider sending the rover to try to get into the pit.

❝ We might take a shot at getting down there, but for a surface rover the odds are not good. ❞ —Red

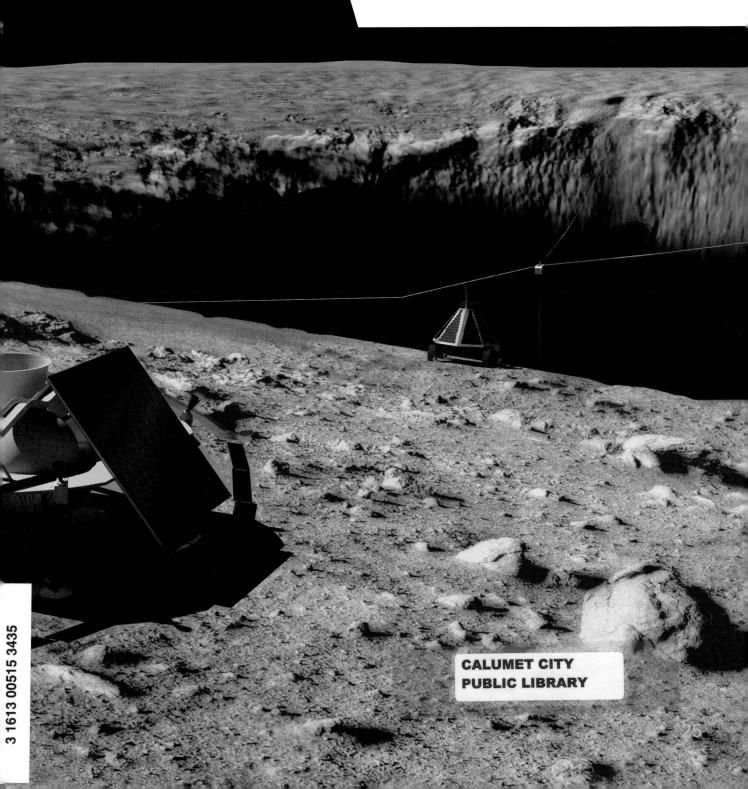

The lander pictured on page 23 releases a pit-scouting rover.

" Robotics today is mostly wheels and motors and driving around and looking a few feet or meters in front of you, to stay out of trouble. " —Red

Inventor feature:
Jules Verne

Whittaker's interest in space exploration was sparked in part by the writings of the science fiction writer Jules Verne.

❚❚ As a kid, I liked a lot of his stuff. Just a couple of years ago, I reread his novel *From the Earth to the Moon* [1865]. It is over 150 years old, but I was quite impressed by how much of the technical detail he got right. ❚❚ —Red

Jules Verne

Jules Verne (1828-1905), a French novelist, wrote some of the first science-fiction stories. Although his books were written before the invention of the airplane, they have remained popular in the space age. Verne forecast the invention of airplanes, television, guided missiles, and space satellites. Verne even predicted their uses accurately.

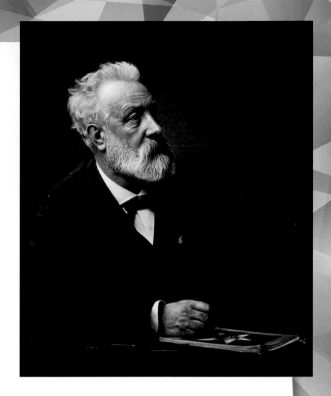

Verne cleverly used realistic detail and believable explanations to support incredible tales of adventure. His fantastic plots took advantage of the widespread interest in science in the 1800's. He carried his readers all over Earth, under it, and above it. Verne's *Twenty Thousand Leagues Under the Sea*, published in 1870, tells about Captain Nemo, a mad sea captain who cruises beneath the oceans in a submarine. In *Around the World in Eighty Days* (1873), Phileas Fogg travels around Earth in the then unheard-of time of 80 days, just to win a bet. Other thrillers include *A Journey to the Center of the Earth* (1864), *From the Earth to the Moon* (1865), and *Around the Moon* (1870).

Stage three:
Descending into the pit

❝ Compared to rolling around on the surface, getting in and getting around inside these pits is a huge challenge. **❞** —Red

The first robot to enter a pit will need to handle some complex **terrain.** At the least, it will need to be able to roll down the rubble-strewn walls of a sloping pit.

❝ The fortunate thing is, robots do a lot better going downhill than they do uphill. **❞** —Red

Still, a pit **rover** will likely require off-road tires and a high *ground clearance*. Ground clearance is the distance from the ground to the body of a vehicle. Vehicles with higher ground clearance can pass over larger obstacles. A pit rover might also trail a tether (cable) connected to an anchor or to its landing craft. If the rover got stuck, it could reel in the tether to back out of rough terrain.

Cavehoppers

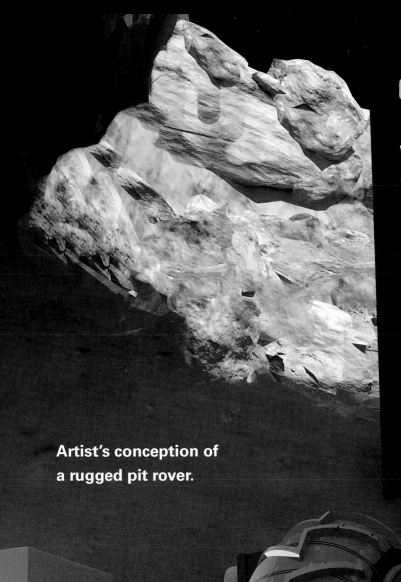

Whittaker's team has also studied the use of robots that can hop over rough terrain and into pits, taking advantage of the lower gravity on such worlds as the moon and Mars. But movement by hopping has proven difficult to control and predict. That makes it easier for cavehoppers to get stranded and harder for them to gather useful data.

Artist's conception of a rugged pit rover.

Big idea:
The Tyrolean traverse

Scrambling down the rubble-strewn slopes of a pit is a pretty difficult challenge. But it may be simple compared to entering a skylight in the roof of a large lava tube. Such a pit might feature overhung walls, requiring a **rover** to *rappel* (lower itself by cable) or drop dozens of feet or meters to the cave floor below.

Whittaker has developed a special robot to explore this kind of pit. He calls it the Tyrobot, because it takes advantage of a mountaineering technique called the Tyrolean traverse. Climbers use the Tyrolean traverse technique to cross an open gap. A cable is strung across the gap and anchored at each end. The climber hangs from the cable and moves along it.

The Tyrobot also moves along a cable anchored between two points. In such a mission, one end of the cable might be anchored to the landing craft. A rover might carry the other end around the pit, anchoring it on the far side. The Tyrobot could then move back and forth along the cable, suspended over the open pit.

This setup enables the Tyrobot to conduct detailed examinations of the pit interior. The robot can move when necessary, taking pictures of features from a variety of angles. It could even use winches (cables attached to drums that are turned by cranks) to lower instruments into the pit. Winches could even be used to lower a rover to the pit floor.

In this artist's depiction, a wall-climbing robot scales a cliff on Mars.

Climbing robots

Researchers are also working to build robots that can climb walls and ceilings in much the same way that the small lizard called a gecko does. Their designs are not quite ready for launch, but a wall-climbing robot might one day open up all kinds of cave **terrain** to exploration.

Inventor feature:
Mother of invention

Red Whittaker's interest in science and technology was nurtured by his mother, June.

❝ My mother was quite ahead of her time. She knew a great deal about science and stars and chemistry. I picked up a lot of that when I was a child. **❞** —Red

In the early 1900's, roles for women in science and industry were greatly limited. But when many men went overseas to fight in World War II (1939-1945), new opportunities opened up for female scientists.

❝ My mother was a chemist in a steel mill in Pittsburgh. Before that, she did an internship at the Mellon Institute [now part of Carnegie Mellon University], where she did a lot of chemistry related to petroleum and oil. **❞** —Red

Whittaker's mother earned a patent as co-inventor of a type of wax used in milk cartons.

❝ She was an extraordinary person. She was even a pilot. ❞ —Red

She flew planes for the Piper Aircraft Company, in Lock Haven, Pennsylvania.

In this 1941 photograph, women pilots for the Piper Aircraft Company salute the airfield officer.

Stage four: Underground exploration

Whether rolling a **rover** down a pit wall or lowering it by winch through a skylight, the goal is to get a rover into an underground cave. To continue exploring from there, the rover will need some special abilities. First, it will have to be able to navigate complex, and unknown, terrain. Second, it will also need a source of energy. Making sure the rovers have enough energy presents many new challenges for Whittaker's team.

❚❚ In exploration, everything is energy. It does not matter whether a rover is turning a wheel, making a sensor observation, computing something, or communicating it. Everything is energy. Everything is power. ❚❚ —Red

Most rovers get their energy from **solar power.** They use devices called solar arrays to convert the energy of sunlight into electric power. Mission planners love solar power because it can be used to easily make the power the rovers need.

❚❚ In the darkness of a cave, there will be no sunlight for the rover to turn into energy. Instead, it will have to carry its own energy. ❚❚ —Red

The first cave rovers will likely be battery powered. They may be able to recharge their batteries using solar power by returning to the cave opening from time to time. But even so, they will have to conserve power as much as possible. They will also have to work in darkness, only being able to see what they can illuminate using conventional lights or **lasers.**

A problem comes up if the cave's walls prevent the cave rover from communicating directly with the outside world. Scientists have thought of several ways to solve this problem. To receive orders or send data, the rover might have to return to the cave opening. Or, the cave rover might drag a cord connected to the lander or the pit descent craft. This cord could provide both power and communication, but it might snag, tangle, and limit the rover's mobility. A Tyrobot or other descent craft might also remain in the cave opening, relaying communications between the rover and the outside world.

Scientists will need to communicate with the rover directly to control its movements. With limited communication from scientists, the craft will have to be able to maneuver and make decisions on its own.

Down to Earth:

ideas from space that could serve us on our planet.

One reason NASA funds out-of-this-world research is that it can result in practical benefits here on Earth. Robots that can operate on their own underground could perform a variety of practical services. Whittaker has designed robots to inspect and service sewer systems. Robots could also play a greater role in mining, helping to reduce some of the thousands of lives lost each year in mining accidents.

Big idea:
Seeing in the dark

❚❚ Here is one example of how you can see in the darkness without using much energy. Instead of shining a steady light, you can take a picture using a camera flash. **❚❚** —Red

In the complex environment of a cave, such an image would show features differently, depending on their distance from the camera.

❚❚ The things that are very close to the camera appear whited out, because they got too much light. Beyond that, there is a sweet spot where you really see some things pretty well. Then at a distance, you do not see anything because it is all dark out there. **❚❚** —Red

You can solve some of these problems by controlling the length of exposure.

❚❚ Using that same flash, you can take a quick picture, a medium picture, and a long-exposure picture. When you do that, at long exposure, things in the distance that had been dark show up. If you take one very quickly, the things that were whited out in the near field can be clear and visible. **❚❚** —Red

Such images can be combined to show features at a variety of distances.

❚❚ What we can do is take 20 different exposures with the same illumination, and then make one image by taking the best range from each and stacking them all together like a loaf of bread. That is one way to see a long distance in the dark with only a little bit of energy. There are a thousand tricks like that. **❚❚** —Red

Three photographs of different exposure lengths have been combined to produce this composite images of a lava tube in Hawaii.

Inventor feature:
Farmer Red

Inventors do not spend their entire lives in a laboratory. They have hobbies and interests just like the rest of us. In his spare time, Red Whittaker runs a farm.

" I am a cattle farmer. I raise cattle and everything that cattle eat. In Pennsylvania, that is corn and oats and barley, but particularly a lot of grass. I also grow grass for hay. " —Red

Whittaker got into farming once his engineering career was already well underway. He suddenly realized he missed his connection to the outdoors.

" I was in a city, in an institution, in a building, in labs, in offices, and I looked out the window, and realized it was a beautiful day. It struck me that I had put aside a lot of the things I really enjoyed, such as being outdoors and doing physical things. " —Red

After thinking about several options, Whittaker decided to give farming a try. He initially committed to giving 10 years to the effort. After 25 years, he is still farming.

Why study caves?

Scientists want to explore alien caves for many reasons. For one thing, caves may offer fairly *pristine* (clean and untouched) environments.

❚❚ Many people do not realize how dusty the moon is. The moon's surface is covered in fine dry dust, like powder. It clings to everything. It gets into moving parts and into the seals on astronaut suits. ❚❚ —Red

The dust forms on the moon's surface, from constant bombardment by tiny rocks called micrometeorites. On Earth, such objects burn up in the atmosphere before they reach the surface. But on the moon, they grind the surface rock over time into a layer of fine powder called *regolith*. Because there is no wind on the moon, the dust does not move around.

❚❚ If you get far enough back into one of these caves, there probably would be no dust from when it was formed and there is no way for dust to blow in. Is it possible that they are pristine and dust-free? If so, these caves could be the only place on the moon not covered with deep beds of dust and rock. ❚❚ —Red

Caves on Mars are even more intriguing. Scientists know that there is water on Mars.

So Martian cave explorers could find water. Scientists also think that the Martian environment may have once been able to support living things. If life ever existed on Mars, it may have survived underground as conditions on the surface grew harsh. Though the odds are slim, a Martian cave explorer could find fossil evidence of living things or even surviving cave life.

Exploration by drone. *Drone* (remote-piloted) aircraft may also serve as a model for future cave explorers. Though the air on Mars is thin, it is thick enough to support specially designed flying craft. Scientists have also experimented with propulsive drones. Such drones move by expelling propellant, in much the same way a rocket does. A propulsive drone could investigate an alien pit and perhaps even enter an alien cave, even in the airless environment of the moon, and gather useful data.

Long-winged drones, such as the one shown at left, may one day fly through Mars's thin atmosphere and study its surface.

Big idea:
future cave dwellers

One of the most exciting reasons to study caves is that they may well provide shelter for future astronauts.

❝ Once upon a time, our ancestors lived as cave dwellers, and for good reasons. ❞ —Red

Caves provided our ancestors with shelter from their environment. In the same way, future astronauts will require shelter from extremes of temperature.

❝ On the surface of the moon it gets hotter than an oven during the day and colder than liquid nitrogen at night. But you go down into a cave and it is a very even temperature, and in many cases quite comfortable. ❞ —Red

Caves can also provide shelter from micrometeorite bombardment.

❝ The biggest challenge to humans exploring beyond Earth is the exposure to radiation from *solar storms* [magnetic activity on the sun]. We were lucky to beat the odds on our short trips to the moon in the 1960's and 1970's. No solar storms occurred. ❞ —Red

Living in caves could shield astronauts on the moon and Mars from such radiation.

Alien cave exploration is still an idea in development. But the future of cave exploration looks promising. Practically every day, new alien caves are being discovered.

In the far future, caves, such as the large one discovered by NASA's GRAIL mission, could be home to a permanent lunar colony of unimaginable size! It is a discovery that truly excites alien cave explorers.

" One of the big surface pits is not too far away, right near the underground cave. There is no way to know for sure if robots could get in. But if they could, it just might transform the future of space exploration. **"** —Red

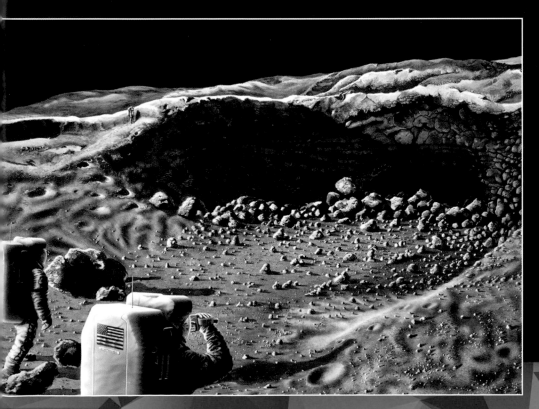

In this painting, astronauts explore a cave on the moon. Such caves may one day provide shelter for lunar colonies.

Red Whittaker and his team

William Whittaker and members of his Astrobotic team.

Glossary

engineer (EHN juh NIHR) a person who uses scientific principles to design structures, such as bridges and skyscrapers, machines, and all sorts of products.

lander (LAN duhr) a spacecraft designed to land on an alien world.

laser (LAY zuhr) a powerful beam of light; also, the machine that makes the beam of light.

mass (mas) the amount of matter in something. Matter is the stuff that makes up everything.

meteorite (MEE tee uh ryt) a piece of stone or metal that does not burn up when it enters the atmosphere around an object in space and falls to the surface of the object.

resolution (REHZ uh LOO shuhn) the ability of an instrument or image to see or show detail.

rover (ROH vuhr) a craft designed to roll around on the surface of an alien world.

solar power (SOH luhr POW uhr) the use of devices called solar arrays to convert the energy of sunlight into electric power.

solar system (SOH luhr SIHS tuhm) the sun and everything that travels around it, including Earth and all the other planets and their moons.

terrain (teh RAYN) an area of land, usually used when referring to the land's surface natural features.

For further information

Want to learn more about caves?

Worlds Beneath Our Feet. Natural Marvels. World Book, 2017.

Want to build your own rover?

Mercer, Bobby. *The Robot Book: Build & Control 20 Electric Gizmos, Moving Machines, and Hacked Toys.* Science in Motion. Chicago Review Press, 2014.

Want to learn what goes into taking an image?

Honovich, Nancy and Annie Griffiths. *National Geographic Kids Guide to Photography: Tips & Tricks on How to Be a Great Photographer From the Pros & Your Pals at My Shot.* National Geographic Children's Books, 2015.

Think like an inventor

Imagine the inside of an alien cave. Is the floor of your cave rough or smooth? Is there water or ice in the cave? Are there boulders or other obstacles? Once you've fully thought about the features of your cave, design a rover that could make its way around your cave.

Index

A

alien caves. *See* robotic exploration of alien caves
astronauts, 40-43

B

batteries, 34

C

Carnegie Mellon University, 7, 32
caves: lava tube, 10-11, 37; solution, 8-9, 11; spelunking, 12-13. *See also* robotic exploration of alien caves
communication with rovers, 35
computers, 15, 18

D

drones, 41

E

Earth, caves on, 8-11
energy for rovers, 34
Evergreen Middle School, 15

F

farming, 38-39
From the Earth to the Moon (Verne), 26

G

GRAIL mission, 20-21, 43
gravitation, 11, 20-21

I

illumination in caves, 34-37

L

landers, 22-25
lasers, 35
lava tubes, 10-11, 37
life, 5, 41
Lunar Reconnaissance Orbiter, U.S., 14

M

Mammoth-Flint Ridge cave system, 8
Mars, 4, 5; descent into pits on, 28-31; lava tubes on, 11; locating pits on, 14-15, 18, 22-26; reasons to study caves on, 6, 40-41, 43
mass, 20
meteorites, 10
micrometeorites, 40, 42
moon, 4-5; caves as shelter on, 40, 42-43; dust on, 40; gravitational mapping, 20-21; human landings, 4, 42; lava tubes on, 11; locating pits on, 14, 18, 22-23

N

NASA Innovative Advanced Concepts (NIAC) program, 7
National Aeronautics and Space Administration (NASA), 7, 15, 35; GRAIL mission, 20-21, 43
National Corvette Museum, 11

P

Piper Aircraft Company, 33
pixels, 18

R

radiation, 42-43
regolith, 40
resolution (optics), 14, 15, 18, 22
robotic exploration of alien caves: aerial and surface craft phase, 22-26; orbital scouting phase, 18-21; overview of, 16-17; past missions, 14-15; pit descent in, 28-31; pit exploration phase, 34-37; reasons for, 4-6, 40-43

rovers, 4, 16; pit exploration by, 28-31, 34-37; pit scouting by, 22-25

S

science fiction, 26-27
sinkholes, 8, 11
skylights (formations), 11, 30
solar power, 6, 34
solar storms, 42-43
solar system, 4-5, 10, 11
spelunking, 12-13
stalactites, 8
stalagmites, 8
stereoscopic images, 19

T

tethers, 28
Tyrobots, 30-31, 35
Tyrolean traverse technique, 30

V

Verne, Jules, 26-27

W

water: forming caves, 8-9; on Mars, 5, 40-41
Whittaker, June, 32-33
Whittaker, William "Red," 6, 7; and team, 44; background and career, 12-13, 26-27, 32-33, 38-39; flash imaging concept, 36-37; on descending into pits, 28-29; on lava tubes, 10-11; on locating caves, 14-15, 18-26; on powering and controlling cave rovers, 34; on reasons to study alien caves, 40-43; on robotic exploration difficulties, 16-17; Tyrobot concept, 30-31
winches, 31, 34
World War II, 32-33

Acknowledgments

Cover	Astrobotic Art by Mark Maxwell
4-5	NASA/Goddard/Lunar Reconnaissance Orbiter
6-7	© J. Helgason, Shutterstock
8-9	© Shutterstock
10-11	ESA/L. Ricci; © Michael Noble Jr., AP Photo
13	© Benjaminjk/iStock
14-15	NASA/GSFC/Arizona State University; NASA/JPL-Caltech/Arizona State University; NASA/JPL/University of Arizona
16-17	NASA
18-19	NASA/GSFC/Arizona State University
20-21	NASA/JPL-Caltech/MIT/GSFC
23-25	Astrobotic Art by Mark Maxwell
27	Public Domain
28-29	Astrobotic Art by Mark Maxwell
31	NASA
33	© Bettmann/Getty Images
34-35	© Shutterstock
37	© Andre Nantel, Shutterstock
39	© Shutterstock
40-41	NASA/JPL/University of Arizona; NASA/Dennis Calaba
43	NASA
44	© Carnegie Mellon University